A Lonely Girl In A Crowded World

Story of a Borderline Personality Disorder Sufferer

Thank you Richard. If it weren't for you and mum, this book wouldn't have been possible.

I love you little brother.

This is a book about how I developed Borderline Personality Disorder, a crossover between psychosis and neurosis, and what it is like for me living with this disorder. I hope that you enjoy it.

Chapter 1: Middle School

I have had Borderline since I was about 9 or 10. Everyone always liked me while I was in my first school, however it was when I moved up to middle school that my problems started. You see I was very badly bullied while I was growing up in middle and secondary school, and this is where my problems stemmed from.

There were three sisters that took a dislike to me the moment they met me. The youngest one was always able to command her older sisters and she used to use my fear against me in horrid ways. There were times that she commanded them to abuse me mentally and physically. The youngest took an instant dislike to me because of these twins I was best friends with at the time. They did not want to be friends with her and chose to stay friends with me, and this put her nose out of joint, metaphorically speaking of course.

Well the bullying was easy enough to deal with for the first year or so, but when I reached year 5, this was when things took a turn for the worse for me.

While I was walking home one day when all of a sudden out of nowhere, the middle aged sister came up behind me with one of her friends, who was also a twin strangely enough, and started hurling abuse at me over something that I had allegedly done to her sister earlier on during school.

Well being the way that I was at the time, decided that telling the truth was the best policy so denied doing any wrong to her sister. She refused to accept this, and we ended up arguing, which then led to her pushing me in front of a car. Luck seemed to be on my side thank the Lord, because one of my neighbors' was walking down the road and she ran out into the road to stop the car before it hit me. There was nothing that anyone could've done to prevent this girl from pushing me, and this was just the start of the terror.

As my school life progressed, the bullying just got gradually worse and worse. I had groups of people being turned against me out of fear of getting the same treatment that I was receiving, and this made me feel awful. I lost all my friends in that school in the space of about 6 months. They had made life so difficult for me to handle, and this was when the voices in my head had started developing. I thought I was going crazy!

I was too afraid to talk to anyone about this because I didn't want people to look at me differently. I had seen people on television that had suffered with voices, and I always believed that something would happen to me if I had confessed to anyone about it.

Being young I did not know anything about mental health problems. I just thought that you were either insane or of sound mind, and at the time I thought I was insane. I suffered in silence, not telling anyone about the bullying, but helping others through theirs, which in turn made their bullies begin to bully me also.

Chapter 2: Secondary School number one

It wasn't until I had moved to my first secondary school that I began to develop friends again. It was supposed to be a fresh start, a clean slate if you will. Never once did I imagine that all of this would follow me and get worse. By this point in time I had had enough of all of it. I knew that if it were to carry on at this school too I wouldn't be able to cope with it all. At the time I knew nothing of suicide, but I was beginning to develop these kinds of thoughts.

For months the bullying carried on in this school, and this time not just with the three sisters. It was like middle school, but ten times worse. The people that were bullying the youngest sister were bullying me, and the three sisters were still doing this also.

In all of my classes in school I was being bullied, singled out in front of the teachers by the students. But the teachers did nothing to help, just stood by and watched as I suffered in their classes.

I had informed the head teacher and the deputy head teacher, and they both accused me of being insane, claiming that nothing was going on and that it was all in my head. Well by this time I was convinced that I was insane.

The voices were getting worse, I was having severe mood swings, I was beginning to change as a person, but through all of this I still helped anyone else that was having trouble. Being able to help someone made me feel a little better about myself, even if only for a split second.

During my time at this school while all of this was happening, I had tried to inform my parents of what was going on and how I was feeling, but it came to a head one night when I wandered into my lounge at home and had written on a big piece of cardboard that I no longer wanted to live. My mother just turned to me and told me to grow up and stop trying to attention seek. She told me to deal with my problems myself.

At the time though my brother was being bullied in the school that I had been in previously, and they must have thought that I was trying to take their attention away from him. However one day when he and I had gone swimming I attempted to take my own life for the first time.

I was swimming and decided that I would try and drown myself; not realizing that the human body has a self-preservation mode built into our brains, and I thought it was actually possible to be able to drown yourself.

My brother bless his soul, was the one who had to pull me up to the surface. Now I would like to say that this was the one and only time that he saved my life, but it wasn't, But we'll get onto that one later.

My parents did eventually start taking notice of what was going on at school with me, and it was like a weight had been lifted off my shoulders, but the only problem was that their way of trying to end it was to get the police involved with it, however this made it ten times worse.

When the police got involved, I ended up being stalked round school, and stalked when I left school by the sisters. With the stalking, it got so bad that I ended up having to run and find my parents because the sisters were strangling my brother and he was turning blue and purple in the face from lack of air, and this was all because he refused to tell them where I was.

My brother has been my knight in shining armour ever since he was a kid, and he doesn't know how much he means to me. He has saved my life more times than he should have.

While I was in school, the bullying in there came to a head when I was sat outside a class one day, and the youngest sister came up to me, told me that her sisters were going to be coming after me during lunch, and I ended up having a major asthma attack underneath the staircase. My cousin who had to call my mum found me shaking and scared, fearing for my life. No one knew just how bad my bullying was.

I put myself through school everyday, walked through those front doors and suffered in silence, never letting anyone know how bad it had become.

However when I went into school three days later, I was in a room with the youngest sister. The teacher had left the room, leaving her and I alone, when she turned round to me and said, and I quote:

"I don't have to touch you to be able to kill you, all I have to do is cause you a major asthma attack, and leave you where no one will find you and without your inhaler and you'll die".

This scared the hell out of me, and that was my last day at that school thankfully

Chapter 3: Secondary School number 2

When I left the first secondary school out of fear for my life, we ended up being moved into emergency accommodation in the next town over. I was home schooled until my parents could get me into a new school. I was so excited. I had reinvented myself by cutting my hair so short that it was just longer than your average male haircut. I had short spiked up hair, and hair colours that varied from brown, to red to purple. None of the students at the school knew me from before, which was perfect for me. I was able to become a new person and forget about the hell I had been through previously. All was going amazingly well for me. I had managed to finish year 8 in my new school, and got to about half way through year 9. Then things went downhill for me.

By this point I was suffering from depression, but had refused to admit anything to anyone about it. It wasn't until I couldn't cope with feeling as low as I was that I eventually told someone about it.

My mum had got me a Doctors appointment to discuss with them how I was feeling, and this was the beginning of my involvement with the mental health services. I explained to the doctor about the voices, which was the first time I had told anyone about them, and I explained to her about the mood swings and the low points I was going through.

I was referred to a counselor in the beginning to see if there was anything that they could do to help me. I have come to the conclusion that the counselors for me did not help when I was young. I was 14 when I first started seeing one, and they treated me like I was 10. This patronized me, and I was lucky enough to have been born with the skill of being able to trick people into believing I was all right.

School life for me was a nightmare in year 9. Not only did I have to deal with the fact that the teachers had let the students know about what had happened to me in my first Secondary school, I was then also having to deal with being called a lesbian for that, and being bullied for being something that I wasn't.

People couldn't quite understand that although I liked women, I wasn't a lesbian as I enjoyed the company of both men and women. This went on right through till I was in year 10. Being called a lesbian I could deal with. It was name-calling and was pathetic compared to what I had already been through in my school life. I just took it with a pinch of salt and brushed it underneath the carpet. The difficult time came for me when I received news from my parents I thought that I would never hear from them. They were back. The sisters.

When I had moved town, and moved school, I had hoped and prayed that I would never have to hear their names mentioned again. But oh boy was I wrong. I was so terribly wrong indeed. Although they never went to the same school as me again, they had moved one road over from where I was living at the time. It was like I could never get away from them, and the memory of the hell that they had put my family and I through. In school I was having enough to deal with because of repercussions from a court case I had going through against the sisters.

The court case was about an attack they had made on my brother and I while we were down the beach. I was so shaken up about that as I thought I would never see them again. It was at this point my parents decided to inform me that they were living one road over from us. At the news of this, my mental health got increasingly worse. I became suicidal again, I was refusing to go out anywhere without being escorted places, I had to give up my paper round in case I bumped into them. But in school, they had managed to infiltrate my circle of friends and turn them against me.

It all came to a head in that school with me regularly bashing my head against a brick wall outside the classrooms in the hope that the voices would leave me alone, but they never did. I was put under a psychiatrist at the local CAMHS services (Child and Adolescent Mental Health Services). The psychiatrist I saw though put me on these antidepressants called fluoxitine (or Prozac they are also known as). These were the worst tablets to have put me on.

I was on them for two months, and each month they had to be increased because they were making me worse, and we did not know why I was getting worse. While I was at hospital I had quite a bad freak out session because my emotions had gotten too high, so I started seeing things that didn't exist, and hearing things that no one else could. I threatened suicide that day just to satisfy the voices in my head. I was put on diazepam that day also to try and calm me down there and then. I went through many different diagnoses when I was a teenager. I was told I had depression; schizophrenia; bipolar, posttraumatic stress disorder, to name but a few.

In regards to the court case, my parents were told either they cancelled it or they would end up having no daughter left on this earth. The court case was ruining my life at school, and making me terrified to leave the house. And their worst fear almost came true.

Chapter 4: Colwood and Father's Day

Father's day was ruined thanks to me. I had by this point in my life had enough of the way that I was. My mental health was getting worse by the day, and so were the hallucinations. At this point I just wanted to end it all and get it over with. I didn't fear death; I welcomed its peace. I had a fear of getting to the point of acting on my thoughts, and the time had arrived when I did. I overdosed in my room on strong painkillers, and wrote a suicide note to my family explaining that it was all getting too much for me, and that I was sorry they had to lose their only daughter for her to find peace again.

I walked out into the living room, well stumbled, and my brother was in there. He was the one who saved my life for the second time in his life, as he was the one who phoned the ambulance and got my parents after reading my note.

When I saw my parents, all I could do was cry because I could feel myself slipping away, and it felt awful while my parents stood there crying and not knowing what they could do.

My mum cried on the phone to the ambulance people because my brother couldn't manage to explain to them what had happened, and this was the first time I ever saw my dad cry.

My dad was a strong man, one who never let his vulnerable sensitive side show to others; but as I lay there dying on our sofa he couldn't contain it any longer.

I spent the week in hospital while they tried to get me a bed in a child and adolescent mental health hospital (a teen psych ward if you will). My parents visited me everyday, but the one person I wanted to see never came to see me. My brother stayed away for the entire time, and never came to Colwood with my parents to collect me for the weekends.

He was the one who had saved my life, and if it weren't for him I wouldn't be here today. I wanted to see him more than anyone, and every day came and I waited.

I waited to see him walk through the hospital doors and hug me. I needed to hear him say that he forgave me for what I had done that day, and every day went but he never showed.

I saw everyone else; my nana and granddad, my aunt, my cousins, even my sister; but never the one I longed to see.

The child psych team came down to see me towards the end of the week to assess my mental health. They asked me a series of questions, and came to the conclusion that it would be best for my safety if I were admitted as soon as possible to Colwood. My mum disagreed because she thought that if I were admitted that I would never want to come back home again, which was true I didn't.

I was terrified of going home and seeing the sisters again, and this was making me worse. But finally when I promised her that I would come home did she agree that I should go in. But unfortunately it was the worst possible time for me to get admitted into there. The day that I was taken to Colwood was my brother's birthday. I felt so horrible because not only had I ruined father's day for my dad, but also I had ruined the one-day a year that revolved around my brother.

For the first few weeks that I was in there, all I could think about was how badly I had hurt my family, and how much I needed punishing for it. I was mentally ill and I had ruined everything all because of three sisters. I wanted blood. I needed to make them pay for what they had done, and this was the thought that kept me going the entire time that I was in there.

But still thinking of this did not make it any easier for me to go home. For the first month I would always say to my nurse that I didn't want to go home, I didn't want her to force me to go home.

I would beg her to make up an excuse for why I had to stay, but every week she would always make me go. She used to tell me that the longer I put off going home, the harder it would become for me to go back.

In my heart I knew she was right, but my head was in protective mode and did not want me going anywhere in case things got worse for me. Eventually I listened to what she had said, and I chose to willingly go home, but this proved my head correct. Things did get worse for me when I chose to go. I was terrified that weekend because my voices were telling me to kill myself again, but when I told one if the on call nurses how I was feeling and that I couldn't go into the kitchen on my own because of it, she told me to go downstairs and make a sandwich with a knife. Worst thing she could've told me to do. I had a rather bad funny turn, and was screaming in fear over something no one could see. That weekend was cut short and I was taken back to the hospital.

After that weekend, they put me under their psychologist there, who was meant to help me find ways of dealing with my head. But if I'm honest, he was the worst psychologist I've ever been to. He was so easy to fool, and I didn't want to be in that place for much longer.

As much as I liked the nurses and the patients in there, I was just getting more and more scared to leave the place for good.

We had monthly reviews with my nurse, psychologist, and my family to see how the progress was coming along, and eventually after about 5 months of being there, they told my family and I that if they could find somewhere new to live that they would allow me to go home for good.

The thought of being able to go home excited me, because it meant that I could see my family every day, but at the same time it scared me half to death because I didn't want to go back home and try to end it all again. But after a month the council managed to move us into emergency accommodation, and so at the next review meeting they agreed to let me out, but on one condition, and that was that we continued our family therapy there.

Chapter 5: round two

A few years passed. I had moved and finished school better than anyone had expected me to, and gone to college for the first time. Things were going well for me. I hadn't had any more episodes, and my mental state was keeping at bay. I was still on anti depressants because they seemed to be the only thing that was keeping me sane. I finished college and hadn't done so well there as everyone had hoped I would've. So I decided to go back to college.

The college I had chosen to go back to was Worthing College. I didn't know anyone here, which was the beginning of the end of my episode free time. I had started there in September, and by October I was back out of that college. I was the eldest student in my classes. Everyone else was about 16, and I was 18 nearly 19. I didn't fit in with anyone, and had no friends there at all. I kept to myself out of fear of things going tits up for me, which I could envision happening.

Everything was going ok until one dreary lunchtime that ruined everything. Someone who had been in my class at school had decided she had also had enough of life, and jumped off the rail tracks next to the college. This threw my head into blind panic because it brought back all the memories from before, and this was something that I did not want coming back to me.

In the end I had to drop out of college, and was put under the travelling day hospital, which was for mental health. My nurse there was perfect for me. She was a great nurse. She helped me through every bad patch that I was having, even explained to me that although I felt insane, that I wasn't.

It was thanks to her that I found out what was wrong with me all along. She was the woman who diagnosed me with Borderline Personality Disorder. She got me all the help that she could. Thanks to my nurse I was put into the STEPPS programme after a year and half of being there, and this helped me tremendously.

It was the work I did in STEPPS that helped me understand my condition, and learn to deal with it. I was taught techniques on how to deal with it, and it taught me that everything I was feeling was normal. I felt like a human being afterwards, instead of a freak of nature.

Chapter 6: Living with BPD

Although I have suffered from this for many years, I still struggle on a daily basis to be able to do simple things that people do. I have to live my life on anti psychotics and anti depressants, otherwise I go downhill big time. I have to cope with mood swings that are so sudden I don't have time to put measures in place to help myself. I have to contend with the voices in my head on a daily basis, which are constantly putting me down and telling me to end it all. I live with my family, and have good friends, but even standing in a room full of people that I know I still feel like a lost little girl who is trying to find her way home. There is nothing that I can do about this, and it is something I will have to contend with every day of my life. There is no cure for BPD, and there is nothing that we can do to help ease the suffering.

People still think that I am crazy, and I still do feel crazy. Every day I wake up and wish that I was no longer here, but then I look over and see my dogs, wagging their tails and happy to see me, and this chases the feelings away. My family help me every day with going out, making sure I'm ok. My mum is the only person in my family who can pick up when something is wrong, and there have been times when she has stopped me from self harming or stopped me from ending it all there and then.

But no matter how hard I try with my life, and how hard I try to fit in and be normal, I always fail. I am covered in scars because of what I went through as a kid. I still cut myself and burn myself.

I feel I have to punish myself every day because of the way that I am, and because of what I did all those years ago. I will be haunted every day of my life with this, but I know that I can help people, and that helps to chase some of the darkness away.

People with mental health difficulties, even depression, get stigmatized and this unfair on us. We are normal people, who are just slightly more unique and special. We have experience on our side, and we can use that to help make sure that others don't suffer in the same way. I know there are people out there who will never change the way that they think about mental health, and that is sad, but there are people out there who would do anything they could to help. I am me, and yes I am different, but I'm still a human being and that is the way I would like to be treated.

I can't go into crowded places out of fear that I will be victimized again. This is the way I live my life now, in fear of people. I still do normal things with people, and I still live my life in a normal way, but the slightest thing can throw me into blind panic, and I don't take change very well.

To live with BPD is difficult, and because it will never go, I will always be this way. I struggle with working, and have to try and find jobs that are not too stressful as stress is one of my triggers.

I still see a counselor even now, after all these years. If it wasn't for them then I would be worse than I am now. I do have periods where I seem ok, and feel better than I normally do, but I know that with these periods there is another bad patch coming up, and this is something that I have to keep an eye out for and prepare for.

But I am who I am, and I will never change. And to be honest I don't think that I would ever willingly change the way I am for the world. I was meant to be this way, and I will use this to help others, and that is the greatest gift I could ever have, the power to help the unfortunate.